CW00728258

This book was made especially for:

❧ HARPER ❧

Dear Harper,

One can't imagine all the places you'll go and amazing things you'll do! Will you build new wonders? Discover new species? Swim in the deepest oceans?

Yes, great adventures lie ahead, and here are 250 words to describe them all. May your life be filled with wonder, magic, and all the good things in this book!

Love,

HARPER *Goes* *on a* SAFARI

crocodile

tortoise

panther

flamingo

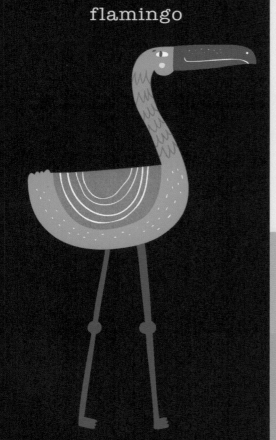

cheetah

gorilla

tiger

monkey

zebra

lion

elephant

gazelle toucan

giraffe

warthog

hippopotamus

All Around
HARPER'S HOUSE

phone

sofa

houseplant

table

chair

teapot

fan

mixer

sewing machine

salt & pepper

clock

television

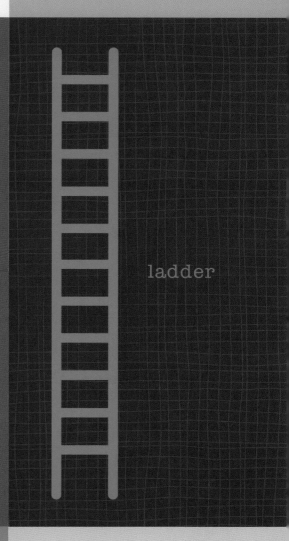
ladder

lamp

armchair

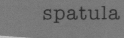
spatula

rolling pin

blender

Time to EAT, HARPER!

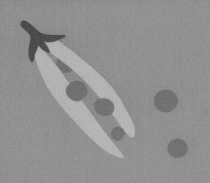

peas

strawberries

lemon

apples

radish

greens

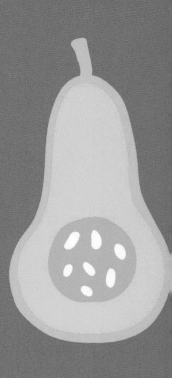

squash

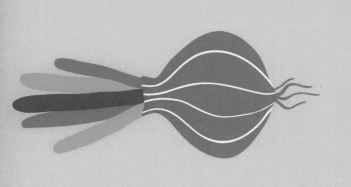 onion

 pear

 tomato

 broccoli

  cucumber

carrot

 pineapple

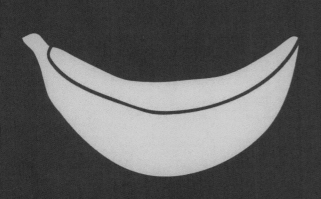 banana

 pepper

HARPER *Visits* *the* OCEAN

jellyfish

message in a bottle

seagull

lighthouse

fish

crab

sea shells

binoculars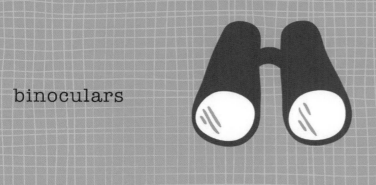

 anchor

 waves

starfish

 coral

seahorse

 helm

whale

boat

HARPER *Is* *on the* GO!

bus

car

fire truck

double-decker
bus

garbage truck

roads

monster truck

convertible

truck

dump truck

airplane

tow truck

hot air balloon

taxi

ambulance

helicopter

school bus

ice cream truck

HARPER *Goes* CAMPING

binoculars

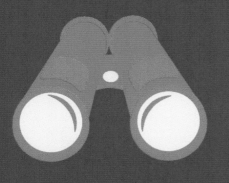

canoe

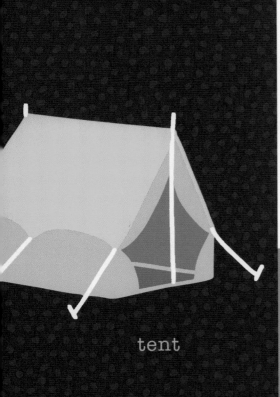

tent

camper

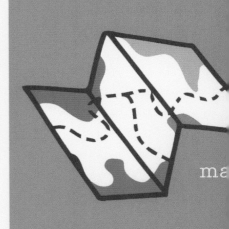

ma[p]

mountains

lantern

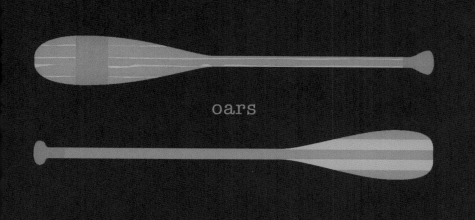

oars

camp chair

fire

compass

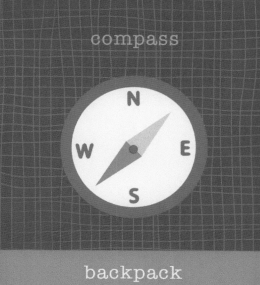

forest

backpack

boots

kayak

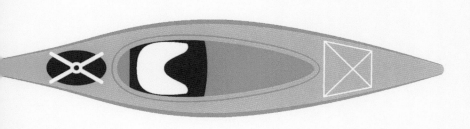

flashlight

What's OUTSIDE, HARPER?

sun

puddle

thunderstorm

cloud

rain

snow

umbrella

thermometer

HARPER *in the* GARDEN

basket

gloves

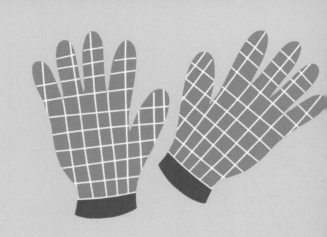

terrarium

pot

boots

hose

watering can

spray bottle

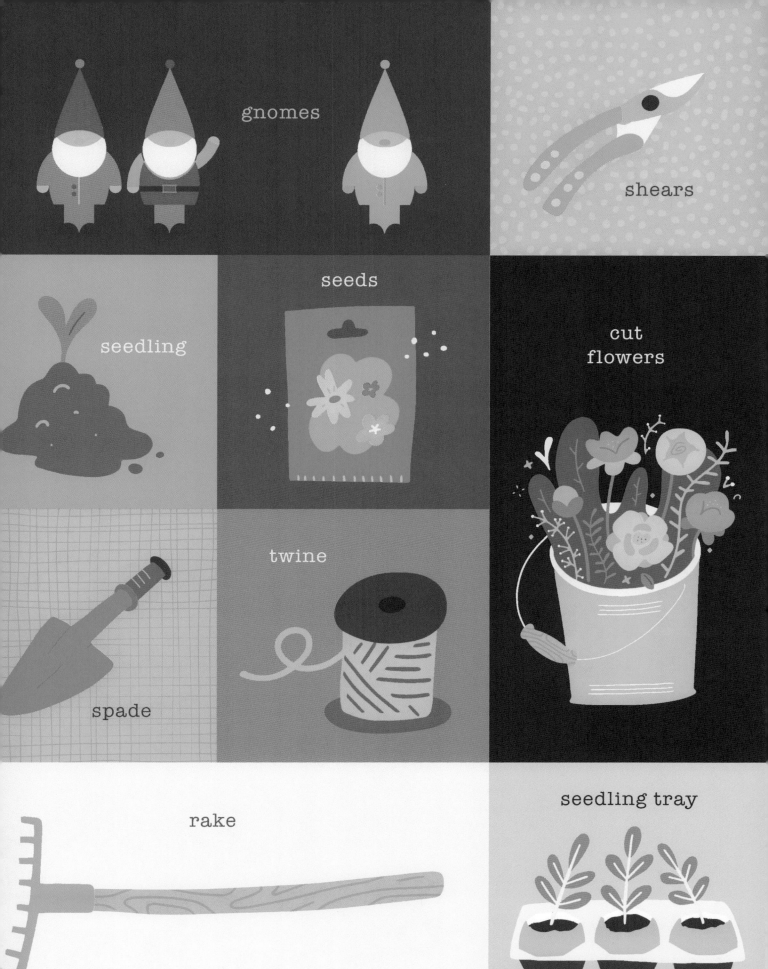

gnomes

shears

seedling

seeds

cut flowers

spade

twine

rake

seedling tray

DINOSAURS *Love* HARPER!

cave

Triceratops

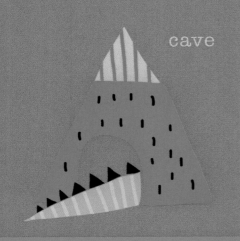

Parasaurolophus

Tyrannosaurus

Stegosaurus

amber

jeep

hat

jungle

volcano

Pterodactyl

Diplodocus

Brontosaurus

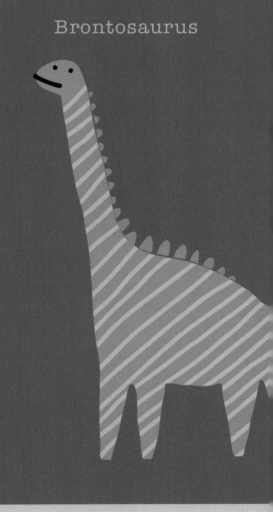

fossils

dinosaur eggs

footprints

Plesiosaurus

What Will
HARPER BUILD?

caution sign

backhoe

front loader

dirt
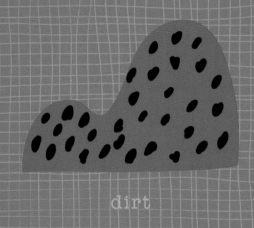

house

forklift

bulldozer

steamroller

water truck

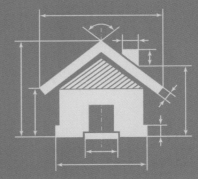

cement mixer

safety cones

crane

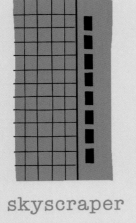

skyscraper

dump truck

construction workers

landscaping

HARPER
in the CITY

park

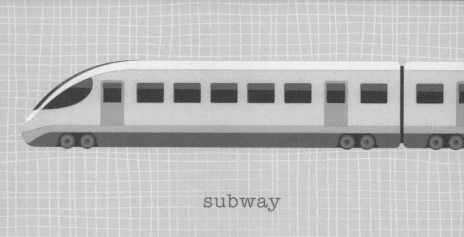
subway

streetlight

city
hall

museum

bus

fountain

crosswalk
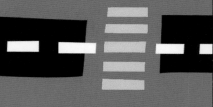

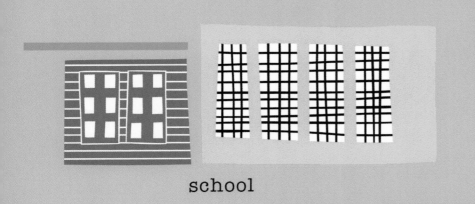

school

store

taxi

police car

apartment
building

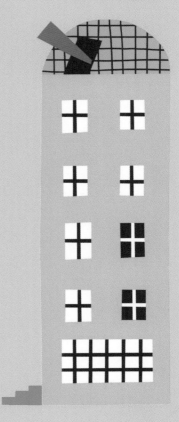

food truck

traffic
light

railroad
tracks

bridge

HARPER *Visits* the FARM

farmhouse

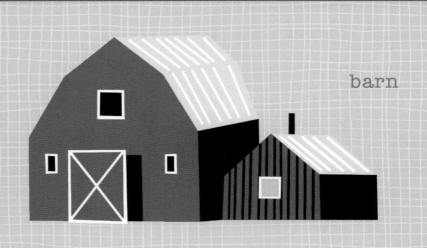

barn

haystack

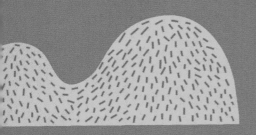

windmill

tractor

cow

plate

fields

chickens

dog

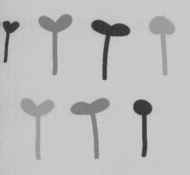

crops

chicken coop

sheep

fences

duck

orchard

pig

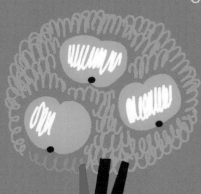

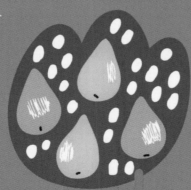

HARPER'S *in a* FAIRYTALE!

ship

unicorn

magic potion

queen

king

fairy godmother

knight

jester

fox

crystal ball

castle

coach

dragon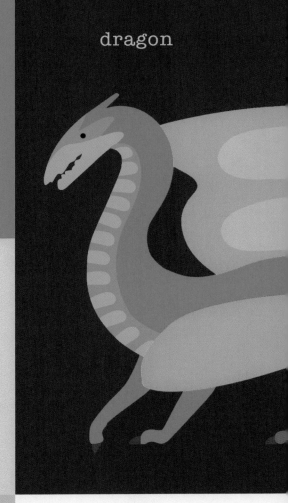

cottage

key

mushroom

mermaid

BATH TIME
for HARPER

soap

towel

rubber duck

toy boat

sponge

plug

faucet

bathtub

conditioner

shampoo

toilet paper

shower

bubbles

soapsuds

comb

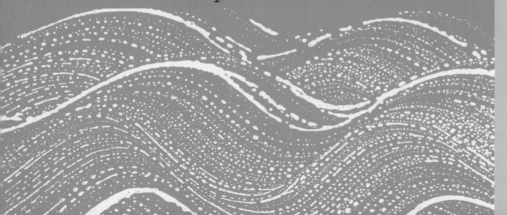

SWEET DREAMS,
Dear HARPER

pillow

moon

bedtime stories

dreams

floss

teddy bear

toothbrush

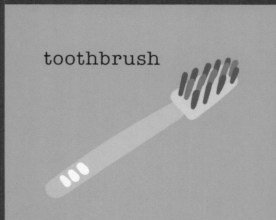

counting
sheep

drink of water

bed

crib

night-light

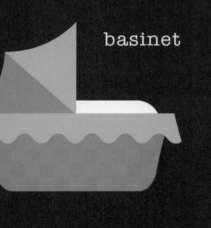

basinet

bunk bed

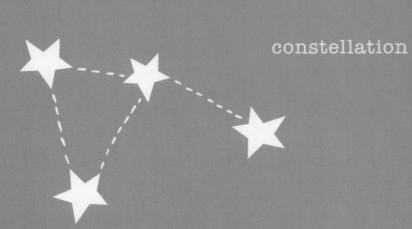

constellation

stars

Copyright © 2020 by Li'l Llama Custom Kids Books

All rights reserved.

Cover and book design by David Miles

Artwork by the following talented Shutterstock artists: Beskova Ekaterina, Bukhavets Mikhail, Aleksandr Trusov, Sharon Silverman Boyd, KNST ART STUDIO, KateChe, tutti-frutti, Svetlana Kharchuk, GoodStudio, Angelina De Sol, katieromanoff_art, Didou, Nadzin, vectorchef, MirabellePrint, JeedChatt, nemlaza, lena_nikolaeva, Afanasia, ArtMari, IYIKON, metel_m, Alena Razumova, EgudinKa, kulyk, Alexander Ryabintsev, solmariart, Ruslana_Vasiukova, Inkley Studio, Incomible, Ira Bagira, Woodhouse, Andrii Bezvershenko, Follow Art, mckenna71, Ira Che, GoodStudio, tandaV, MG Drachal, Macrovector, Wondermilkycolor, Ksenia Zvezdina, Victor Z, momoforsale, vectortatu, Carboxylase, Kwirry, Buravleva stock, reddish, DoozyDo, Maike Hildebrandt, lyeyee, babystardesign, Kiarnight, Kataryna Lanskaya, Popmarleo, judilyn, Fresh Take Design, NotionPic, NadineVeresk, Sudowoodo, Angelina De Sol, twobears_art, Vector pro, lena_ nikolaeva, Olga Zakharova, NadineVeresk, jsabirova, and PinkPueblo.

Printed in Great Britain
by Amazon

24606156R00021